A Family in Thailand

This book takes you on a trip to Thailand, in southeast Asia. From the capital city, Bangkok, you will travel to Ayutthaya, which is close to the Pomwat family's home. Jaran Pomwat works in a sawmill on the banks of the River Chao Phraya. You will visit his home and meet the rest of his family. You will discover how they live, what their hobbies and interests are, and what they like to eat.

FAMILIES AROUND THE WORLD

A FAMILY IN
THAILAND

Peter Otto Jacobsen and
Preben Sejer Kristensen

The Bookwright Press
New York · 1986

Families Around the World

A Family in Australia
A Family in China
A Family in France
A Family in Holland
A Family in Hong Kong
A Family in Iceland
A Family in India
A Family in Ireland

A Family in Japan
A Family in Mexico
A Family in the Persian Gulf
A Family in Switzerland
A Family in Thailand
A Family in the U.S.S.R.
A Family in West Africa

First published in the United States in 1986 by
The Bookwright Press
387 Park Avenue South
New York, NY 10016

First published in 1985 by
Wayland (Publishers) Limited
61 Western Road, Hove
East Sussex BN3 1JD, England
© Copyright 1985 Text and photographs
Peter Otto Jacobsen and Preben Sejer Kristensen
©Copyright 1985 English-language edition
Wayland (Publishers) Limited

ISBN 0–531–18038–7
Library of Congress Catalog Card Number: 85–71726

Phototypeset by Kalligraphics Limited
Printed by G. Canale and C.S.p.A., Turin, Italy

Contents

Flying to Thailand

Our journey to meet a family in Thailand, takes us first to Bangkok, the exotic capital of this Far-Eastern country. Thailand is situated in southeast Asia. It is about the size of France and the countries it is bordered by are Burma, Laos, Cambodia, and Malaysia. Its name means

Bangkok, the busy capital of Thailand, and the center of the communications network nationwide.

"Land of the Free."

We are flying to Don Muang airport which is north of Bangkok. As we emerge from the cloud we see below us the rice paddies of the central plains. This is the country's major rice-producing area, irrigated by the great Chao Phraya River.

As we step out of the plane we are hit by the very hot, humid atmosphere. It's early May and just at the beginning of the rainy season. It can be as hot as 35°C (95°F) in Bangkok, at this time of year.

We leave the airport by bus and drive the 19 kilometers (12 miles) to the center of Bangkok. We are traveling along a new road, which was opened in 1982, called the Bagna-Port Expressway. It takes you from the airport directly to the coast, avoiding the city by going over it! We turn off and make our way to our hotel in the busy center of Bangkok.

Thailand covers an area of 500,000 sq km (193,000 sq mi).

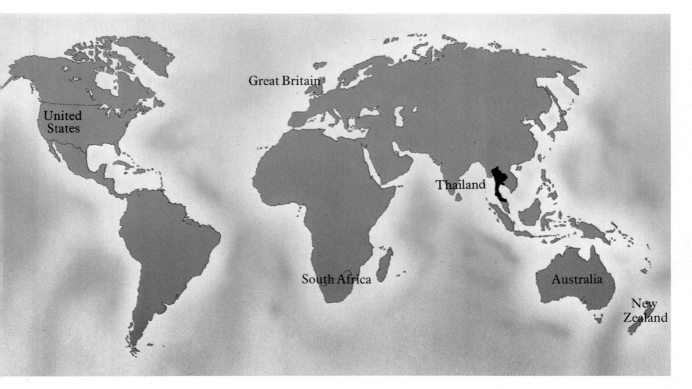

A day in Bangkok

We get up very early the next morning to explore the city. Bangkok has been the capital of Thailand since 1782, when the ruling Chakri dynasty was founded by the king, Rama I. The present king, Bhumibol Adulyadej, is one of his descendants. The old name for the city was Raltanakosin.

Bangkok is famous for its traffic jams, so we decide to travel in the old-fashioned way – on the canals. We want to visit the floating market, which is open every day, early in the morning. The canals become busy with sampans, overflowing with exotic fruits like mangoes, bananas and

The early morning floating market in Bangkok, where traders are busy.

pineapples, brought in from the country-side. Other Thai delicacies are for sale too, like dried beef or dried fish. People, wearing wide-brimmed straw hats, sit cross-legged in the bottom of the boats, jostling together, competing for custom.

We leave the market and move on along the canals to get a better view of the city. Bangkok used to be known as

A typical wooden house on stilts, on the banks of the canal, with storage space beneath it.

the "Venice of the East," because of its network of canals. Most people lived on the edge of the canals and all trade was carried out in sampans. As we go along we see many of the old wooden houses on stilts. They are still lived in.

9

The Grand Palace in Bangkok.

We stop to visit the Wat Arun, the Temple of the Dawn, which stands at the waterside. This is one of the 300 magnificent Buddhist temples in Bangkok. Buddhism is the main religion in Thailand. All of the temples are beautiful from the outside, as well as from the inside, with glittering roofs and spires. The oldest of these is Wat Phra Kaeo, where the Emerald Buddha, a statue carved out of solid jade, sits on a throne 10 meters (34 feet) high. This is the most revered statue of the Buddha in the country. There is an important ceremony held three times a year, when the robes of the statue are changed. This ceremony can only be carried out by the king of Thailand. He dresses the ancient figure in robes which are appropriate to the season. The Thai people recognize three different seasons – the hot, the rainy and the cold seasons.

We return from our trip in time to go and see some Thai boxing. This is a traditional national sport and involves using feet, elbows, and knees, as well as fists. Music is played during the fighting, on long drums and cymbals. The boxers are superstitious and so they wear charms for protection and good luck during the fight. The crowd gets very excited and people shout and jump up and down throughout the match.

The statue of the Buddha at Wat Mahathat, one of the many temples in Bangkok.

By train to Ayutthaya

A statue of the reclining Buddha at Ayutthaya.

The following day we take a train to Ayutthaya, which is the town near the Pomwat family's home, 70 kilometers (43 miles) away. Ayutthaya was once the capital of Siam (Thailand's old name) and was founded in 1350. But in 1767 it was invaded by the neighboring Burmese and destroyed.

The train makes its way through the countryside of orchards and rice paddies.

Rice is Thailand's biggest crop and much of what is grown in this area is exported.

To grow rice a lot of water is needed. The plain around Ayutthaya is flooded with water from the River Chao Phraya. This great river is also used for transportation of rice in barges to the port at Bangkok, as well as for moving timber from the northern forests to the sawmills. A lot of people live in this area because here they can make a better living than in the north.

The train is pulling into the station in Ayutthaya. We get off and find a taxi to take us to meet Jaran Pomwat.

Below: *Part of the ruins of the old capital of Ayutthaya.*

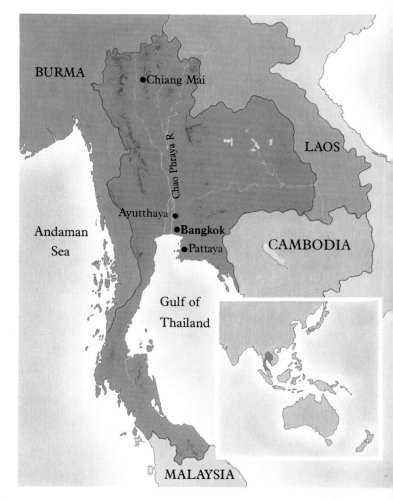

Above: *The map shows how Bangkok's position at the mouth of the river was important for the defense of the old capital.*

13

Working in a sawmill

We meet Jaran Pomwat at the sawmill where he works. We see that there are hundreds of sawmills next to each other on the banks of the river.

"Nearly half of Thailand's 500,000 square kilometers (198,000 square miles) is covered with forest, mostly of hardwoods like teak," Jaran Pomwat tells us. The timber comes from the north and is transported by river, or road to the sawmills. Outside the sawmills there are thousands of tree trunks piled up together. It is an impressive sight.

"In the old days," Jaran says, "elephants used to help with the forestry. Nowadays, it is mostly done by machines. Sometimes, on particularly

Jaran sits on one of the thousands of tree trunks piled up outside the sawmill.

The circular saw cuts up the timber into planks.

difficult ground, elephants are still used to move the tree trunks."

Jaran takes us into the mill and shows us where he works. He uses a circular saw to cut the trunks up into planks. "There are about 200 people working here, and there are as many women as there are men. The women move the planks out of the mill on to the waiting trucks," he says.

Some of the timber produced here is sold abroad. "Thailand exported much more teak in the past than it does nowadays. In this country other types of trees are used more often than teak. Redwood costs only half as much and is popular for building and furniture-making," he explains.

We leave the mill and drive the short distance to the Pomwats' home.

Meeting the Pomwat family

The Pomwat family in their living room.

We walk along a path between tall grasses and trees, with Jaran leading the way. The Pomwats' house is built on the side of the broad Chao Phraya, the River of Kings. Four small rivers which rise in the hills in the north of Thailand, merge to form the Chao Phraya. It is Thailand's most important river.

The Pomwats' house is built on stilts because of the danger of flooding, and is made of wood from the local sawmills. Beneath the house there is space enough for keeping hens and ducks. There are several similar houses nearby, with ladders leading up into them. We take our shoes off at the bottom of the ladder and climb up after Jaran. Taking your shoes off before entering a house, or temple, is a Thai custom.

Pensri, Jaran's wife, greets us warmly, holding Pontip, their three-year-old daughter. Prasit and Tornygoo, Pensri's parents, greet us too. They live in the house as well. We all sit down on the floor in the main room and talk. The house is small and so we are squeezed in between the partition wall around the bed and the other end of the house. The kitchen is separated from the main room by another partition. Through the open windows we have a view down the river, where we can see the family's boat tied up at the water's edge. We can also see several girls standing in the river, wearing sarongs, washing their long black hair. The sarong is worn both by men and women in the Far East. It does not matter that their clothes get wet as they dry so quickly in this climate.

Jaran built the house himself, with wood from the local sawmills.

Jaran Pomwat

Jaran Pomwat is 38 years old and has been working at the sawmill for several years. His working day starts at 7:30 a.m. and finishes at 5:30 p.m.

"I work six days a week for a daily wage of 45 baht. If I work on a Sunday I get double pay," he tells us. "I also get six consecutive days holiday each year, as well as thirteen other days. These days coincide with the Buddhist holy days."

We ask Jaran if he is religious. He nods. "Every morning the monks come sailing down the river from the monastery, and I always give them either money or food. Once a week I go to the temple to pray to the Buddha."

We ask Jaran to tell us more about the Buddha. He says, "The Buddha means 'The Enlightened One,' and was the name given to an Indian Prince called Sidhatta Gotama who lived 600 years before the birth of Christ. He was not a god and never claimed to be, but he was a teacher. He taught people a way to lead their lives in peace and happiness. His disciples are the monks, called *bhikkus*, who carry on his teachings here and all over the world."

Jaran tells us that there are many Buddhist festivals throughout the year. "They celebrate particular events in the Buddha's life. Apart from celebrations in the temples, there are candlelit processions through the streets with music and dancing. For Loi Krathong, the Festival of Light, which happens in November, candles are floated on the canals of

Jaran thinks that the ideal wife should be kind, economical and a good cook.

Bangkok, in beautiful banana-leaf and lotus-petal cups."

But the most sacred festival is Vaisakha Puja, which marks the birth, enlightenment and death of the Buddha, and occurs on the day of the full moon in May. "On this day I walk around the temple three times carrying a lighted candle. I never really think about my religion. I think I probably follow it just because I am a Thai."

A Buddhist monk paddles down the Chao Phraya River, in the early morning.

Pensri Pomwat

Pensri is 26 years old. She and Jaran have been married for five years.

"When we first met, Jaran was infatuated with me," she tells us. "He proposed to me but I refused him. So he went to my father. My father then came to me and told me that I should marry Jaran. After that I could not refuse."

Pensri spends most of her time looking after Pontip and running the home.

"Jaran gives me his wages every two weeks, and I do all the shopping. With the help of my mother I do all the cleaning, washing and cooking as well. I have no other job. I find that the housework and looking after Pontip takes up nearly

Pensri spends nearly all her time looking after Pontip and running the home.

Pensri crochets brightly colored clothes for Pontip in her spare time.

all my time."

Pensri has several hobbies. She knits and crochets clothes for Pontip, in brightly colored wools.

"I also have a kitchen garden, which all the family help me with. We grow bananas, coconuts, lemons and chillies."

We ask her what she thinks the ideal husband should be like. "He should be hard-working and earn enough money to provide for his family," she replies.

Family life

Prasit feels that everything has become more expensive, but fishing is still free.

Prasit, Pensri's father, is the oldest member of the family. He feels that progress has not been all it could have been during his lifetime. "Everything has become more expensive, although as a family we cope well, economically," he tells us. "But, despite the huge antenna on the roof, we haven't yet got a television," he adds, laughing.

Tornygoo, his wife, earns a little money as a masseuse. Massage is a long-established art in Thailand.

"It involves rubbing and kneading parts of the body to improve the circulation and suppleness," she says. "The process can take several hours and is not always a comfortable experience."

Tornygoo helps her daughter run the household. They go together to the local market to do the shopping. She also enjoys looking after her grandchild, Pontip. Pontip will not go to school until she is 6 years old.

"A national program of education was introduced in 1960," Jaran tells us. "It required children under 15 to complete six years of elementary education. Secondary education lasts five years, but few finish this. Those who do finish can go on to one of fifteen universities."

In the evenings Pontip goes to bed after the family has eaten together. She sleeps with Jaran and Pensri in a huge hammock, which is one of the two beds in the house. Pensri explains that Jaran

Tornygoo helps her daughter in the house and earns a little money as a masseuse.

made it so that it would take up only a little space in their small house.

Prasit and Jaran enjoy going out fishing together.

"We go fishing from the boat, or just from the bank," Prasit explains. "Jaran fishes with bait but I always use a net. I have learned a special technique."

"There are plenty of fish in the river," Jaran adds, "and we often catch enough to feed the whole family. But our boat is very old and fills up with water, so we have to bail it out before we set off."

Jaran asks us if we will stay and have supper before making our way back to Ayutthaya. We readily agree.

Left: *Jaran bails out the old boat.*
Below: *There are two beds in the house; one of them is a hammock, which Jaran made.*

Mealtime

Tornygoo and Pensri go to the market together, to do the shopping.

We are sitting together on the floor in the main room when Pensri brings in the supper. It is dark outside now, and it feels warm inside the small wooden house.

We are about to eat the family's favorite dish, Pat Preeowahn. This is made with fresh shrimp, pineapple and garlic. "I fry up all these ingredients together for a few minutes with some chillies, small cucumbers, tomatoes and onions. We usually serve it with rice," Pensri tells us. "I leave the tails on the shrimp, so they are only half-peeled. The dish looks very pretty," she says. Jaran goes and fetches us water from a large jar, in the corner of the room. It is rainwater that has been collected, and is the family's only source of drinking water.

We all talk together over the meal and Jaran says to us, "I think that the most important thing for a family and a good marriage is that we all understand each other."

We ask Pensri what she wants for Ponip. "She shall have a good education and then marry a man who can provide for

Pensri prepares the meal sitting on the floor.

Jaran fetches some drinking water for us from an earthenware jar.

her. I don't mind whether she makes good use of her education or whether she looks after a home and family, as I have," she says.

It is getting late. We tell Jaran that we must leave. He shows us to the door and shines a flashlight onto our shoes at the bottom of the ladder. We thank the family for the delicious meal, and for spending their time with us. Then we climb down the ladder, collect our shoes and wave our goodbyes to the Pomwat family.

This is Pat Preeowahn and rice – a mixture of shrimp, chillies, tomatoes and cucumbers.

Facts about Thailand

Size: 500,000 sq km (193,000 sq mi)
Capital city: Bangkok.
Population: At the end of 1983 the population of Thailand was 49,515,000.
Language: Thai is the official language. Chinese and English are also spoken.
Money: The currency is satang and baht. 100 satang equal 1 baht.
Religion: The national religion is Buddhism. There are also small percentages of Muslims, Christians, Hindus and Sikhs.
Climate: The climate is tropical, with high temperatures and humidity. Average temperatures range from 20°C (68°F) in December to 37°C (98°F) in April.
Government: Thailand is a constitutional monarchy with King Bhumipol Adulyadej as Head of State. There is a National Assembly made up of the Senate and the House of Representatives. Members of the Senate serve for six years and members of the House of Representatives serve for four years.
Education: The Government has taken responsibility for establishing and supporting a national school system. Elementary education is compulsory for six years. Secondary education continues for a further five years. There are fifteen state universities, as well as many technical and teachers' training colleges.

Agriculture: Thailand is primarily an agricultural country. Of its working population, 80% work on the land. Major exports are rice, rubber, corn, teak and tapioca. Other crops for the home market include, cotton, coconuts, sugarcane, fruit, vegetables and tobacco.
Industry: Thailand's major industries include the manufacture of construction materials, iron, steel, electrical goods, plastics, car assembly, rice mills and sawmills.

Glossary

Bait Something you put on a hook at the end of a fishing line to attract the fish.

Cymbals A musical instrument, consisting of a pair of plate-like pieces of brass which are clashed together.

Disciple Someone who is a follower of another person's teachings, often religious.

Dynasty A ruling family, whose right to rule is passed on through generations.

Hardwood Timber taken from slow-growing trees, which are not evergreen.

Irrigation A means of bringing water to dry areas of land, through channels.

Jade A valuable hard stone, usually green in color.

Masseuse A woman who practices massage.

Monastery A large building where monks live.

Paddy A flooded field planted with rice.

Sampan A small wooden boat, moved by oars.

Sarong A shirt-like piece of clothing, worn by men and women in the Far East.

Superstition Belief in magic, or fear that is not based on scientific truth.

Teak A hardwood tree used in making furniture.

Index

Acknowledgments

All the illustrations in this book were supplied by the authors, with the exception of the following: Tourism Authority of Thailand 6, 10; Camerapix/Hutchison Library 8, 9, 11, 12, 13; John Topham Picture Library 19. The maps on pages 7 and 13 were drawn by Bill Donohoe.